John Johnston

Diary Notes of a Visit to Walt Whitman and Some of His Friends, in

1890

With a series of original photographs

John Johnston

Diary Notes of a Visit to Walt Whitman and Some of His Friends, in 1890
With a series of original photographs

ISBN/EAN: 9783337015619

Printed in Europe, USA, Canada, Australia, Japan

Cover: Foto ©ninafisch / pixelio.de

More available books at **www.hansebooks.com**

DIARY NOTES OF

VISIT TO WALT WHITMAN

AND SOME OF HIS FRIENDS, IN 1890.

WITH A SERIES OF ORIGINAL PHOTOGRAPHS.

BY

JOHN JOHNSTON, M.D. EDIN.,

HONORARY SURGEON TO BOLTON INFIRMARY,
AUTHOR OF "MUSA MEDICA."

MANCHESTER:
THE LABOUR PRESS LIMITED,
ARKWRIGHT MILLS, MILLER STREET.

LONDON:
THE "CLARION" OFFICE, 72, FLEET STREET.
1898.

TO

J. W. WALLACE.

"SOMETHING FOR A TOKEN."

PREFACE.

The following Notes, extracted from a Diary record of a visit to America, in July, 1890, were written at the time, mainly for a small group of friends, referred to as "The Eagle Street College," and without any idea of publication.

They were afterwards printed in pamphlet form, for private circulation, and a copy having been sent to Walt Whitman, he not only endorsed them, but requested that copies should be sent to a large number of his friends. (See letter on page 147).

Their reception among these and others interested in Whitman having been so favourable, and requests for copies so frequently coming to hand, it is now decided to give them complete publication, with the addition of some of the photographs taken during the visit.

It has also been thought best to let them go as they were originally written; so that, whatever they may lack in literary form, they may present, in the most direct and perfect manner possible, the actual impressions of the time.

In this way, it is hoped that they will preserve a certain life-likeness which might otherwise be lost. And, anyhow, it is the method which Whitman himself approved, as will be seen by the following. On January 9th, 1891, he wrote to me:

"Next time you write give me a list of whom you have sent the *Notes* to. (I think you have builded better than you knew.)"

At the celebration of his seventy-second birthday at Camden, N.J., on May 31st,

PREFACE.

1891, a handsomely bound and illustrated copy of the pamphlet, with illuminated inscription, was presented to him from me, whereupon he said:

"Say, you fellows, who dabble in the bigger streams of literature, there is a splendid lesson that such notes as these of Dr. Johnston teach. It is the same lesson that there is in the play of the 'Diplomatic Secret.' At the end of that interesting play, which I have seen, a great fellow who is in pursuit of it comes in, crying, 'At last I have found it—I have found the Great Secret! The Great Secret is that there is no secret at all!' That is the secret. The trick of literary style! I almost wonder if it is not chiefly having no style at all. And Dr. Johnston has struck it here in these *Notes*. A man might give his fame for such a secret."

Later on, during the same evening, referring to the same subject, he said:

"Who can doubt the Doctor's American reports? Even those who doubt me, doubt the 'Leaves,' ought to see how superbly the Doctor handled his material—or let it handle itself."

J. J.

Bolton, 1898.

CONTENTS.

	PAGE.
First Interview	21
Second ,,	45
Third ,,	69
Fourth ,,	78
Additional Notes	89
Visit to Brooklyn—	
Andrew H. Rome—John Y. Baulsir	93
Visit to West Hills—	
Sandford Brown	105
Visit to Herbert Gilchrist	118
Visit to John Burroughs ..	121
Supplementary Notes	146

INDEX TO PHOTOGRAPHS.

	PAGE.
Frontispiece	6
Mickle Street, Camden, N J	19
Walt Whitman's Room	29
Walt Whitman's House *facing page*	42
Walt Whitman on Camden Wharf	49
Walt Whitman and Warry Fritzinger on Camden Wharf	55
Interior of Downstairs Room in Whitman's House.. *facing page*	68
The "Fulton" Ferry Boat	97
West Hills, Long Island—Whitman's Birthplace	103
John Burroughs	123
Interior of John Burroughs' Study	135
Reduced *Facsimile* of Portion of Whitman's Letter	147

A Visit to Walt Whitman.

On Tuesday, July 15th, 1890, I landed at Philadelphia—"the city of brotherly love,"—and after getting through the troublesome Customs, I called at the post-office, where I found a letter from Mr. Andrew H. Rome, of Brooklyn, inviting me to go and stay with him, and enclosing a letter of introduction to Walt Whitman. Crossing the ferry by the ferry-boat *Delaware*, I arrived at Camden, putting up at the "West Jersey" Hotel, and about noon I walked down to Mickle-street, which I

My Arrival at Philadelphia.

Mickle **Street,**
Camden.

found to be a quiet and retired side street, grass-grown on the roadway and side walks, and ornamented with two rows of large and graceful, leafy trees, which give it quite a pleasant, breezy, semi-rural appearance. The houses are, for the most part, quaint, half-timbered structures, painted different low-toned colours, and of various heights and outlines.

Number 328—which, by the way, is duplicated next door—is an unpretentious, two-storied building, with four wooden steps to the front door, on which is a small brass plate engraved " W. Whitman." I rang the bell, and the vestibule door was opened by a fine young nautical-looking man, of whom I enquired if Walt Whitman was at home. On his answering " Yes," I gave him my

MICKLE STREET, CAMDEN, N.J. × Walt Whitman's House

card, and was shown into a room on the left side of the lobby—a sort of parlour, with the blinds three-parts closed against the heat. The young man informed me that "Mr. Whitman was pretty well, but had been rather sick." He "would see if he would receive me." He returned almost immediately, and asked me to "go right upstairs, turn to the left, and go straight in."

I did so, and before I got to the room I heard a voice from within calling, "Come in, Doctor! Come right in!" and in another moment I was in, and saw Walt Whitman seated. Stretching forth his right hand as far as he could reach, he grasped mine with a firm, affectionate grip, saying, " Glad to see you. I've been expecting you. Sit down."

My First Interview.

I did so, and his next words were, " And how are you ? " To which I replied, and he continued, " You find it very warm in these parts, don't you ? Strangers often find it uncomfortably so, but I just resign myself to it, and take things quite easy, and I get along pretty well during the hot spell. So you've been travelling about our States, have you ? "

" No," I said, " I only landed in Philadelphia this morning."

" Ah, I am confounding you with another friend of mine."

And so he talked on in the most genial, natural, and affable manner for a few minutes, until I said, " But I'm forgetting my letter of introduction, and my commission." This gave me the opportunity of changing my seat from facing the light to a place by the window, where I could see him better. I then handed him Mr. Rome's letter, and while he was reading it I took a look at him and his surroundings.

The first thing about himself that struck me was the physical immensity and magnificent proportions of the man, and, next, the picturesque majesty of his presence as a whole.

Walt Whitman's Appearance.

He sat quite erect in a great cane-runged chair, cross-legged, with slippers on his feet, and clad in rough, grey clothes, and a shirt of pure white linen, with a great wide collar edged with white lace, the shirt buttoned about midway down his breast, the big lapels of the collar thrown open, the points touching his shoulders, and exposing the upper portion of his hirsute chest. He wore a vest of grey homespun, but it was unbuttoned almost to the bottom. He had no coat on, and his shirt sleeves were turned up above the elbows, exposing most beautifully shaped arms, and flesh of the most delicate whiteness. Although it was so hot, he did not perspire visibly, while I had to keep mopping my face. His hands are large and massive, but in perfect proportion to the arms; the fingers long, strong, white, and tapering to a blunt end. His nails are square, showing about an eighth of an inch separate from the flesh. But his majesty is concentrated in his head, which is set with leonine grace and dignity upon his broad, square shoulders; and it is almost entirely covered with long, fine, straggling hair, silvery and glistening, pure and white as sunlit snow, rather thin on the top of his high, rounded crown, streaming over and around his large but delicately-shaped ears, down the back of his big neck, and from his pinky-white cheeks and top lip over the lower part of his face, right down to the middle of his chest; like a cataract of materialised, white, glistening vapour, giving him a most venerable and patriarchal appearance. His high, massive forehead is seamed with wrinkles. His nose is large, strong, broad, and prominent, but beautifully chiselled and proportioned, almost straight, very slightly depressed at the tip, and with deep furrows on each side running down to the angles of the mouth. The eyebrows are thick and shaggy with strong white hair, very highly arched, and they stand a long way above the eyes, which are of a light blue with a tinge of grey, small, rather deeply set, calm, clear, penetrating, and revealing unfathomable depths of tenderness, kindness, and sympathy. The upper eyelids droop considerably over the eyeballs, the left rather more than the right. The full lips are partly hidden by the thick, white moustache. The whole face impresses one with a sense of resoluteness, strength, and intellectual power, and yet withal, it evinces a winning sweetness, unconquerable radiance, and hopeful joyousness. His voice is highly pitched and musical, with a *timbre* which is astonishing in an old man. There is none of the usual senile tremor, quaver, or shrillness, his utterance being clear, ringing, and most sweetly musical.

But it was not in any one of these features that his charm lay so much as in his *tout ensemble* and the irresistible magnetism of his sweet, aromatic presence, which seemed to exhale sanity, purity, and naturalness, and exercised over me an attraction which positively astonished me, producing an exaltation of mind and soul which no man's presence ever did before. I felt that I was here face to face with the living embodiment of all that was good, noble, and lovable in humanity

Before I refer to his talk with me, I may say a word about his surroundings, which were unique. All around him were books, manuscripts, letters, papers, magazines, parcels tied up with bits of string, photographs, and literary *materiel*,

His Surroundings.

which was piled on the table a yard high, filled two or three wastepaper baskets, flowed over them on to the floor, beneath the table, on to and under the chairs, bed, wash-stand, etc., so that whenever he moved from his chair he had literally to wade through this sea of chaotic disorder and confusion. And yet it was no disorder to him, for he knew where to lay his hands upon whatever he wanted, in a few moments.

His apartment is roomy, almost square, with three windows—one blinded up—facing the north. The boarded floor is partly carpeted, and on the east side stands an iron stove with stove pipe partly in the room. On the top of the stove is a little tin mug. Opposite the stove is a large wooden bedstead, over the head of which

WALT WHITMAN'S ROOM.

hang portraits of his father and mother. Near the bed, under the blinded-up window, is the wash-stand, a plain wooden one, with a white wash-jug and basin. There are two large tables in the room, one between the stove and the window, and one between that and the wash-stand. Both of these are piled up with all sorts of papers, scissorings, magazines, proof-sheets, books, etc., etc. Some big boxes and a few chairs complete the furniture. On the walls, and on the mantel piece, are pinned or tacked various pictures and photographs—Osceola, Dr. Bucke, Professor Rudolph Schmidt, etc., etc.

He himself sits between the two windows, with his back to the stove, in the huge cane chair,*

---

* –since described by himself in a letter to me as "the big, rattan, heavy-timbered, old yellow chair"–

which was a Christmas present from the children of Mr. Donaldson, of Philadelphia, and was specially made for him.

Raising his head from Mr. Rome's letter, which he read with the aid of a folding vulcanite-rimmed *pince-nez*, he said:

His Talk.
"Oh, Doctor, you did not need an introduction to me; but I am very glad to hear from my old friend Andrew Rome. You know he was my first printer, with his other brothers, and I have a deep regard for them."

He talked so freely, and so unconstrainedly to me for over an hour, that I cannot possibly note down all that he said; and the following are mere scraps of his most intensely interesting talk :—

" That must be a very nice little circle of friends you have at

Bolton." I assented, and he went on—"I hope you will tell them how deeply sensible I am of their appreciation and regard for me; and I should like you to tell all my friends in England whom you come across how grateful I am, not only for their appreciation, but for their more substantial tokens of goodwill. I have sometimes thought of putting my acknowledgments in print in some form or other. I have already alluded to it, but I feel it deserves more. I have a great many friends in England, Scotland, and Ireland, but most in England. I hope I acknowledged your and Mr. Wallace's communications—some of my correspondents are rather remiss, and I do not wish to be on the list of defaulters at all."

This gave me an opportunity of

presenting him with the book and letter which my friend J. W. Wallace had kindly commissioned me to give him. The book was Symonds's " Introduction to the Study of Dante," and while reading the letter he exclaimed :

" How wonderfully distinctly Mr. Wallace writes ! "

" Yes," I said, " and he speaks just as distinctly as he writes."

" Ah, that is one of his characteristics, then. It is a pleasure to see such beautiful writing. Sometimes one has to wrestle with handwriting."

Reading on, he exclaimed, " Have you met Symonds ? "

" No," I replied.

" He is a great friend of mine," he continued, " never seen, but often heard from ; and he has given me a good many of his books from time to time. He writes a good deal, and writes well; and he reads my books."

Reading further on, he said, "What a wonderful eye Mr. Wallace has for the beauties of external nature—the light, the sky, the earth." (This was in reference to a sentence in J. W. Wallace's letter beginning, "I draft this in the open fields.") "That used to be a kink of mine. 'Leaves of Grass,' was mainly gestated by the sea shore, on the west coast of Long Island, where I was born and brought up. There is a great deal of sea there."

I here mentioned that I purposed visiting Long Island and Huntington. "You do!" he exclaimed, evidently pleased; "then you must go to West Hills. It is a very picturesque place, and is still occupied by the same family, named Jarvis, that succeeded my father and mother in the farm. It is rather a common name there, and I think it must be a corruption of some old English name."

"Do you know Gilchrist?" he then asked.

"No," I said, "but I have an introduction to him, from Captain Nowell, of the *British Prince*. I believe he is staying on Long Island."

"Yes," he answered, "quite close to Huntington. He is located there, and you must go and see him."

Here I handed him J. W. Wallace's beautiful letter to me the day before my departure. As he read it, he exclaimed, "The dear fellow!" At one part of it he was visibly affected—tears standing in his eyes—and for a few moments he did not attempt to speak.

Upon my saying that I intended going to Timber Creek, he said, "That is a place I am very fond of. You must, while there, go and see Mrs. Susan Stafford, at Glendale, three miles from Timber Creek. She is a great friend of mine. Tell her that you have seen me, and that I am still, as I say, holding the fort."

On my saying that I might call on John Burroughs, he took up his big pen and wrote out the address on one of his envelopes, as well as that of Dr. Bucke, whom he suggested I should visit, if possible.

"Do you know Robert Ingersoll?" he asked me.

His opinion of Ingersoll.

"Only by repute," I replied.

"He was at your banquet, according to the report in the paper you sent me."

"Yes," he said, "and made a good speech of over an hour long. He lately sent me a copy of one of his books, most beautifully got up. Here it is," handing it to me, and showing me the inscription on the fly-leaf. "He is a wonderful man —one of those men who remind me of the ancient Peripatetics, who used to deliver long orations in a manner which few nowadays can. In Ingersoll there are none of the stock tricks of oratory, but it flows from him as freely as water, pure and clear, from a hidden spring which eludes all the investigations of chemistry. It has spontaneity, naturalness, and yet behind it *everything*."

But he checked himself, saying,

"I'm talking too much, and infringing on the doctor's orders, and I may have to pay for it by some little prostration."

This led him to again refer to his physical condition, which we had spoken of at the beginning of the interview.

His Health and Habits.

"I am fairly well, for me, at present, though I have been sick lately. I live very simply. I had breakfast on bread and honey— there's some of the honey up there," pointing to a butter-cooler half buried in the pile of papers on the table.

On my tasting it, he remarked, "It is in the comb, just as the good friend who lives where the bees make it sends it to me. Isn't it delicious? You can almost taste the bees, can't you? Then I'm very fond of blackberries and fruits generally. I have two meals a day; breakfast at half-past nine, and dinner at four o'clock. I get out into the open air every day, if possible; my nurse (the young man I had seen downstairs) wheels me out in the cool of the evening, and I get along wonderfully well. My physical functions are fairly regular, and my mental faculties are unaffected, except that they are slower than they used to be. The brain has been somehow wounded—I don't know the exact physical condition—I doubt if even the doctors know—but my mentality is still as good as ever, with the exception of its being slower than formerly."

I here referred to his paralysis.

"Yes," he said, " my right arm is my best, but I have a good deal of power in my left."

He then held it out for me to feel, which I did, and I was surprised at the wonderful softness and pliancy of the skin, and the firmness and fulness of the muscles beneath.

As I thought I had stayed long enough I rose to go, when he said: "I wish I could give you something. Have I given you my picture? I suppose so."

I replied that he had not, and, glancing round, I saw a torn scrap photograph of himself among the pile of papers, and held it towards him.

"Ah," he said, "that's torn, but if you care to have it you may. I'll write my name on it."

And, taking up his huge pen, he wrote on it, "Walt Whitman, July 1890."

Before leaving him I happened

to mention my copy of "Leaves of Grass," whereon he expressed a desire to see it, and asked me to "come again to-morrow," and show it to him, which I consented to do.

I also mentioned that I had seen a copy of the first edition of "Leaves of Grass" (the thin, quarto copy which Mr. Cuthbertson, of Annan, has), and that we were anxious to possess it.

"Why?" he asked.

"Because," I replied, "we know that the type had been partly set up by your own hand, and the book showed the first inception of your ideas."

"As to the printing," he said, "that edition was on very little different footing from the others. I always superintended, and sometimes undertook part of the work

WALT WHITMAN'S HOUSE.

myself, as I am a printer, and can use the 'stick,' you know.'"

Shaking hands with him, I came downstairs and was invited by Mrs. Davis, the housekeeper, to sit down in the front room, which is less than the one upstairs and is evidently the visitors' reception room. The most striking thing about it is the large collection of photographs and portraits that adorn it. Among these I noticed oil paintings of his father, his mother, and himself. The mantelpiece is covered with photographs, among which are those of Dr. Bucke, the late Mrs. Gilchrist, Mr. Herbert Gilchrist, and others· Curiously enough, I found a portrait of J. W. Wallace, and a copy of my photograph of Ecclefechan, as well as one of myself, which we sent to him, three years ago. His

His Room Downstairs.

wheeled chair occupies one corner, and his big house-chair the other. Two statuettes of ex-President Cleveland and a huge head of Elias Hicks stand in separate corners.

His Household. In the room I found a little coloured girl, Annie Dent, "cleaning Mr. Whitman's wheeled chair," as she said. The young man who wheels him out and attends upon him, and whose name is Frederick Warren Fritzinger — " Warry," Whitman calls him—is a fine-looking young fellow with beautifully symmetrical features, coal-black eyes and hair, and a quiet, unobtrusive, gentle manner. He is a genuine " sailor boy," as Whitman says. His father was a sea-captain, and he has been most of his time at sea, having been round the world three times.

Mrs. Davis — Warry's foster mother and the widow of a sailor who was drowned at sea — is an extremely pleasant and comely young "ma'am," almost typically American in face and speech, in striking contrast to Warry, who speaks without the least American accent. She has been with Whitman for six years, and Warry about three. They are both evidently very fond of him. During my stay they gave me a good deal of detailed information respecting his habits and mode of life, and were extremely kind to me in many ways. After chatting awhile I bade them good-day and left the house.

In the evening I had another good hour's talk with Whitman — an unexpected treat. At 7 p.m.

My Second Interview.

he was wheeled by Warry right past my hotel, according to his custom, down to the wharf, close to the river. As I was waiting about with my camera in the hope of meeting him, he accosted me, and I accompanied them down to the river's edge. As we approached the wharf he exclaimed, "How delicious the air is!"

On Camden Wharf.

On the wharf he allowed me to photograph himself and Warry, (it was almost dusk and the light unfavourable), after which I sat down on a log of wood beside him, and he talked in the most free and friendly manner for a full hour, facing the golden sunset, with the cool evening breeze blowing around us, the summer lightning playing on our faces, and the ferry boats crossing and re-crossing the Delaware.

AND SOME OF HIS FRIENDS.

Soon a small crowd of boys collected on the wharf edge to fish and talk, which elicited the remark from him that—

"That miserable wretch, the mayor of this town, has forbidden the boys to bathe in the river. He thinks there is something objectionable in their stripping off their clothes and jumping into the water!"

American Boys.

In reference to these same boys he afterwards remarked:

"Have you noticed what fine boys the American boys are? Their distinguishing feature is their good-naturedness and good temper with each other. You never hear them quarrel, nor even get to high words. Given a chance, and they would develop the heroic and manly, but they will be spoiled by civilization, religion, and the damnable conventions. Their parents will want them to grow up genteel—everybody wants to be genteel in America—and thus their heroic qualities will be simply crushed out of them."

His Talk on the Wharf.

Among his other remarks were something like the following:

Referring to his services during the war, he said that the memories of the American people were "very evanescent." "I daresay you find the same thing in England"—this without the slightest tinge of resentment or ill-feeling in his words; in fact, I never heard him express an angry feeling except when he referred to the mayor's action in reference to the boys, and to the influences which he knew would spoil them for men.

WALT WHITMAN ON CAMDEN WHARF.

The great hope of the America of the future, he said, lies in the fact that fully four-fifths of her territory is agricultural, and must be so; and while in towns and cities there is a great deal of pretentious show, sham, and scum, the whole country shows a splendid average, which is an absolute justification for his fondest hopes, and nothing could ever destroy it. All his experiences of the war confirmed him in it, and it was yet destined to find a full fruition in the future.

He quoted the saying of the Northern Farmer of "Lord Tennyson" as he called him—"Taake my word for it, Sammy, the poor in a loomp is bad"; which he took exception to, saying that the poor in a lump were not bad. "And not so poor either, for no man can become truly heroic who is really poor. He must have food, clothing, and shelter, and," he added significantly, "a little money in the bank too, I think."

"America's present duty," he continued, "was to develop her material sources for a good many years to come, and to trust that the spirit of the men who fought as those soldiers did would yet prove itself and justify our most sanguine hopes." He repeated, almost *verbatim*, the "Interviewer's Item" in "Specimen Days," the gist of which is that it is the business of the Americans "to lay the foundations of a great nation in products, in agriculture, in commerce," etc., and "when these have their results and get settled, then a literature worthy of us will be defined." Unlike other lands, the "superiority and vitality" of the nation lies not in a class, a few, the gentry—but in the bulk of the people. "Our leading men," he says, "are not of much account, and never have been, but the average of the people is immense, beyond all history." In the future, he thinks, "we will not have great individuals or great leaders, but a great average bulk, unprecedentedly great."

Speaking of the war, he said that the surgeons, with whom he mixed a good deal, proved themselves heroic in their struggles to save the lives of the soldiers of both sides. "My sympathies," he said, "were aroused to their utmost pitch, and I found that mine were equalled by the doctors'. Oh, how they *did* work and wrestle with death! There is an

His reference to the American War.

impression that the medical profession in war time is a bit of a fraud, but my experience contradicts this, and nothing can ever diminish my admiration for our heroic doctors." I remarked that he had not put this in his book so emphatically, to which he said that he knew he had not, but felt that he ought to do, and if opportunity offered he intended doing so.

O'Connor and he, with a few others "who," he said, "must have been something like your little band in Bolton," were among the few in Washington who supported Lincoln in his policy: "We are ready enough to shout hurrah for him now, but I tell you that up to his death he had some very bitter enemies."

"There were times, too, when the fate of the States trembled in

WALT WHITMAN AND WARRY FRITZINGER ON CAMDEN WHARF.

the balance—when many of us feared that our Constitution was about to be smashed liked a china plate. But it survived the conflict. We won, and it was wonderful how we *did* win."

Referring to Warren, as his "sailor boy," he said that he had been of great service to him when he was at a loss about the names, etc., of parts of a ship. It had always been his custom, when writing or describing anything, to seek information directly from the men themselves, and he gave me two illustrations of this. *Re "Leaves of Grass."*

1. In one edition of " Leaves of Grass " he wrote, " Where the sea-whale swims with her calves," because he had often heard sailors say that the calves did swim with the mother; but on reading it to an old whaler he was told that it

was a very exceptional thing for a whale to have more than one calf, so he altered it to—" Where the sea-whale swims with her calf." (See " Leaves of Grass," p. 56).

2. He was under the impression that the Canadian raftsmen used a bugle and he referred to it in one of his lines; but when he went to Canada he found his mistake, and struck it out in the next editon.

Speaking of Walter Scott's Edition of " Leaves of Grass," he said he did not like it. "It was like cutting a leg, or a shoulder, or the head off a man, and saying that was the man." He preferred that people who wished to read him should have *the whole critter*, and those parts of his book to which so many took exception, were the very ones that he regarded as most indispensable.

"Voltaire," he said, "thought that a man-of-war and the grand opera were the crowning triumphs of civilization, but if he were living now he would find others more striking in the modern development of engineering, etc."

"A ship in full sail is the grandest sight in the world, and it has never yet been put into a poem. The man who does it will achieve a wonderful work." "I once cherished the desire," he continued, "of going to sea, so that I might learn all about a ship. At another I wished to go on the railway to learn the modern locomotive. The latter I did to some extent, but the former I did not."

I asked him where I could get a copy of Dr. Bucke's "Man's Moral Nature." He told me at Mackay's, Philadelphia, and on my asking whether I could get a copy of John Burroughs's "Notes" there also, he said, "Oh, *I* will give you a copy of that, if you like. I think I have one I can spare."

In the Street. After listening to his delightful talk—(oh, that I could reproduce his words, and, more than all, the sweetness of his voice, the loving sympathy, the touches of humour, the smile that played round his lips and in his merry twinkling eyes, the laughter that shook his stalwart frame, and the intense magnetism of his personal presence!)—we returned, I accompanying him right to his own door in Mickle Street. He talked the whole time, seemed pleased with everything and everybody, and everyone, man, woman, and child seemed to like him. He saluted nearly every person he passed—

the car drivers he accosted by name; to the young men, he said "How do, boys?"; to the women sitting on the door steps, with babies in their arms, he said, "How do, friends, how do? Hillo, baby!" The labourers loafing at the corners saluted him with "Good evening, Mr. Whitman!" and some took off their hats to him, though most simply bowed respectfully.

As we went along he told me that he had "sent off a card to Wallace," and continued, "When you see him tell him what a pleasure it is for me to see his beautiful caligraphy. I get so many letters that I can only read with a struggle, that I cannot help stopping to admire one which is well written. I am very fond of a well printed book. Your William

Black & Sons, of Edinburgh, produce some splendidly printed works I think I was intended for an artist; I cannot help stopping to look at the 'how it's done' of any piece of work, be it a picture, speech, music, or what not."

"Ingersoll is a good illustration of what I mean. From my point of view the main question about his matter is, 'What does it amount to?' But I cannot but admire his manner of giving it utterance—it is so thoroughly natural and spontaneous, just like a stream of pure water, issuing we know not whence, and flowing along we care not how, only conscious of the fact that it is beautiful all the time."

On his Doorstep.

Soon we reached his house, where Warren "scotched" his chair in the angle between the steps and the wall. He invited me to take a seat beside him on the steps, which I did, and he talked off and on for half-an-hour longer, mostly about his health and physical condition. He allowed me to feel his pulse, which I was pleased to note was fairly full and strong, and quite regular —no intermission, as I half expected. Upon my expressing the hope that he would not feel any bad after effects from to-day, he said—

"No, Doctor, I don't think so, though I have had quite a number of visitors. A dear niece (my brother's daughter) came to see me, after a considerable interval, and I have had several others as well as yourself, Doctor. It has been quite a 'field day' with me. My doctor is very strict, but I am always fearful of being too good, you know, and I am often tempted to trespass." He then told me the following story:—

An old gentleman, named Gore, lived opposite to him (in Mickle Street), who was so strictly proper in all his ways that once, when ill, he asked the doctor so many questions about what he must eat, drink, and avoid, that the doctor told him the best thing for him would be to go on a "devil of a drunk"! "By which," said Whitman, "I guess he meant that he lived so strictly by rules, that it would be best for him to break through and away from them all for once. And" he added, with a chuckle, "I sometimes feel that way myself!"

"I suppose after this I shall have what Oliver Wendell Holmes calls 'a large poultice of silence.' Holmes is a clever fellow, but he is too smart, too cute, too epigrammatic, to be a true poet."

"Emerson came nigh being our greatest man; in fact, I think he is our greatest man."

Some people passing and saluting him, I said, "You seem to have lots of friends about you, Mr. Whitman."

"Yes," he replied, "and I have some very bitter enemies. The old Devil has not gone from the earth without leaving some of his emissaries behind him."

He then referred to the lines he wrote—at the request of an editor—upon the death of the old German Emperor, and said that his Democratic and Liberal friends were incensed at him for venturing to say a word in his favour.'

"You know, I include Kings, Queens, Emperors, Nobles, Barons, and the aristocracy generally in my net—excluding nobody and nothing human—and this does not seem to be relished by these narrow-minded folks."

"I had a visit last year from a young English earl, who, in the course of conversation, said:—

"'I have an impression that you regard lords and nobles as akin to fools.'

"'Well,' I replied, 'there is an impression of that kind abroad.'

"'But,' said the earl, 'I venture to hope that you may be

---

* The following are the lines referred to:—

THE DEAD EMPEROR.

To-day, with bending head and eyes, thou, too, Columbia,
Less for the mighty crown laid low in sorrow—less for
    the Emperor;
Thy true condolence breathest, sendest out o'er many a
    salt sea mile,
Mourning a good old man—a faithful shepherd patriot.

willing to admit that there may be exceptions—that they are not *all* alike!'

"Which I thought," said Whitman. "a remarkably good answer."

As it was now 9 p.m. (his bedtime), I bade him good night, and went to my hotel, pondering deeply on many things, and marvelling at the wondrous magnetic attraction this man had for me—for I felt I could stay with him for ever.

Wednesday, July 16th.—A magnificent day, but so intensely hot that movement of any kind is almost impossible. It was my intention to go to Timber Creek to-day, but as I find that it is not very easy of access, and the temperature being so oppressive, I resolved to spend the time

Another Day at Mickle-street.

at 328, Mickle-street instead. I am glad that I did so, because I have been able to take photographs of the house and its inmates, and have held much pleasant converse with them. Mrs. Davis gave me an engraved portrait of Whitman, and expressed a great desire to send something as a little present to my wife. She is an altogether agreeable person, and so charmingly natural that I do not wonder at Whitman liking her; while Warren is so gentle, so unassuming, frank, intelligent, and unaffectedly kind-hearted, that the more I see of him the better I like him. He and I had quite a long chat and a stroll, which I enjoyed very much, and all he told me served but to deepen my reverential regard for my majestic

INTERIOR OF DOWNSTAIRS ROOM IN WHITMAN'S HOUSE.

old hero. He said that two years ago the doctors—including Dr. Bucke, who was in attendance—all said that he could not live, but that he is better now than he was for a long time after that. He always attends to his mail himself, and replies with his own hand to all his letters, except those of autograph hunters, which are consigned to the waste-paper basket.

But my good fortune did not end here, for I was favoured with another brief interview with Whitman himself, whom I found lying upon his bed (over whose head hangs a large daguerrotype of his mother, another of his father hanging by the washstand), fanning himself—prostrated by the intense heat. I took the fan and fanned him for about five minutes, when he said,—

My Third Interview.

"I have found that copy of John Burroughs's 'Notes,' and I will get up and give it to you."

I assisted him on to his feet, and with his right arm round my neck and my left round his waist we walked across the floor to his chair, wading through the sea of papers on our way.

He then gave me John Burroughs's little book, and taking up two other booklets, he said,—

"I wish you to give these to Mr. Wallace, and these"—(taking up two similar ones)—"are for yourself."

They were copies of "Passage to India" (1871), and "As a Strong Bird on Pinions free" (1872).

I thanked him, and afterwards, at my request, he kindly wrote our names and his own on the title pages of them all.

As I did not want him to talk much, I showed him some of my photographs. One of Annan, from the Milnfield, he especially admired, saying—

"What a beautiful vignette! There's nothing finer. It is very pretty."

He looked at it with evident interest for several minutes, and though I intended it for John Burroughs I gave it to him.

He was interested in my copies of "Leaves of Grass" and "Specimen Days" (Wilson and McCormick's), which he had not seen before, but he at once recognised the type, and said,—

"I see they have used our type and their own title page. I believe they had permission to do so."

When shewn the photograph of

the interior of "Eagle-street College," he exclaimed,—

"So this is the room where you good fellows all meet! What a beautiful room!"

I asked him if he recognised the portrait on the wall.

"Is it mine?" he asked eagerly; "which one is it?"

I told him that it was published in the *Illustrated London News*, when he said,—

"Oh, I have seen it, and I don't like it."

"Why?" I asked.

"A friend of mine says there's a foxy, leering, half-cynical look about it, and I think he's right," he replied. "It's a wonderfully good piece of engraving, though," he added.

I gave him a photo of J. W. Wallace's room, as well as those of

J. W. W. himself, which I took in his room.

He referred to our hour on the wharf last night with evident pleasure.

Soon rising to go, I said, "Is that the portrait of Osceola?" referring to an old tattered engraving tacked on the wall near the door.

"Yes," he replied; "do you know much about him?"

"Not much," I said. He then gave me a brief sketch of Osceola's history, telling me that he was a Seminole chief, whose grandfather was a Scotsman, married to an Indian squaw down Florida way, and when trouble broke out some fifty years ago he was basely betrayed, imprisoned, and literally done to death.

"That portrait," he continued, "is by George Cable, who is quite a clever portrait engraver. I got it in Washington during the war. It was packed away for a good many years, and when I found it it was all torn, cracked, and frayed. I spent an hour one day in piecing it and pasting it on that paper."

Among the photographs on the mantel upstairs I noted the original of the engraving in my edition of "Leaves of Grass," two of Prof. Rudolph Schmidt, of Copenhagen, one of Dr. Bucke, and others.

"And that," I said, pointing to a picture behind a pile of papers, "is another oil painting of yourself?"

"Yes," he said, "do you like it?"

"I do," I replied, hesitatingly.

"Then you may take it with you if you like; I don't care for it," he said. "It was done several years ago by Sidney Morse, but I don't think it is satisfactory."

"Nor do I. In fact, I've never yet seen a portrait of you that is quite satisfactory to my mind," I said. "They are portraits, but they are not *you*."

"No, I guess not," he said. "You cannot put a *person* on to canvas—you cannot paint vitality."*

Before leaving, he again referred to his circumstances, saying that he got along pretty well. The time of his extreme poverty had gone. He had many good friends, his wants were few, "and," he added, but without the least touch of sadness, "it will probably not be for very long that I shall want anything. I have no desire to emulate

---

* This portrait, one of the few oil paintings of Whitman, and of Jovine proportions, is valuable, as shewing something of the colour and freshness he retained even in advanced life.

the manners of the *genteel*, and I never was one to whom so-called refinement, or even orderliness, stood for much."

Feeling that I had trespassed too much, and quite overwhelmed with his generosity, I took my leave.

On the mantel of the room downstairs I found the photograph of " The Boys of the Eagle-street College," as well as those of Carlyle's grave and birth-room, which we had sent to him.

In the evening, I walked down to the wharf, in hopes of seeing Whitman and " Warry," but was disappointed. I sat down on a log, and ate my repast of fruit and crackers. Near me were a good many boys, of the lower middle class, fishing and frolicking, and I could not but remark the genuine good humour that prevailed among them, and the entire absence of anything approaching to rudeness or bad language; joking, of course, there was, but all in good-natured fun, and I never heard a single unseemly utterance. I think our English boys of a similar class would compare very unfavourably with them. Nurses, with babies and little children, were sitting about the logs, and I enticed one bright little boy of three-and-a-half years on to my knee with my bag of crackers. The sun had just set over the river, and Venus had risen in the crimson afterglow. I stayed there, in the waning light, enjoying the cool breeze from the Delaware, until the mosquitoes drove me home.

Thursday, July 17th.—Another

day of magnificent sunshine and intense heat.

I crossed the Delaware in the *Weenonah*—Whitman's old favourite ferryboat, he told me the other night, while we were sitting together on the wharf—the name of an old Indian tribe, though probably a a corrupt spelling.

My Fourth Interview.

Returning, I took a bag of fruit with me to Mickle-street, and received a most cordial welcome from my dear old friend, whom I found sitting in his chair fanning himself, looking quite bright and happy, dressed as on my first visit, and spotlessly clean. He gave me his manly grip with extended arm, saying—

"How do, Doctor, how do? Take a seat "—pointing to a chair. He said he had had a fairly good night, and had partaken of his usual breakfast of bread and honey (with milk and iced water, I think).

In a few minutes he said, "I'm going to send this photograph to Wallace"—lifting up a large mounted photograph from the top of his pile of papers—"I wish him to substitute it for the one he has hanging in his room, as I don't like that one at all. It makes me look, as I told you, a bit foxy, sly, smart, cute, and almost Yankee. So if you will take this one, and ask him to put it in place of the other, I shall be glad. If it doesn't quite fit the frame you can get what we call a matt—I dare say you in England have them—and make it fit."

The Gutekunst Portrait.

I said that Wallace would value this photograph very highly indeed, and I considered it the very best one of him I had yet seen.

"Yes," he said, "I think it is

pretty satisfactory myself. They got me over in Philadelphia, much against my inclination, in the spring, I think it was, and that is the result of my sitting. Nowadays photographers have a trick of what they call 'touching up' their work —smoothing out the irregularities, wrinkles, and what they consider defects in a person's face—but, at my special request, that has not been interfered with in any way, and, on the whole, I consider it a good picture. And now I'll write my name on it, and I want you to take it to Wallace with my love." He then wrote on it, "Walt Whitman in 1890."

I told him I should try and copy it.

"Oh!" he said. "Well, if you do, I should be glad if you would send me a copy." This I promised to do.*

I now produced my bag of fruit, and gave him an orange, which he at once put to his nostrils, saying, " How delicious it smells ! "

He smelled it in silence three or four times, each time dwelling upon it, and taking long, deep inspirations, closing his eyes, and being apparently lost to everything except the delicious feeling which the aroma of the luscious fruit imparted to him. I noticed that he did not do this with any fruit except the orange, and that grapes, peaches, and pears were admired and commented on, but not handled so lovingly or fondled over, as the orange, which he again took up and smelled after putting all the others aside.†

---
*A reduced copy of it forms the frontispiece to this volume.
† He is endowed with exceptionally acute senses. Dr.

He then took up a little volume —"Camden's Compliment to Walt Whitman "— saying, " Oh, I've found a copy of that little book I spoke of the other day, and will give it to you since you say you've not seen it."

Now it so happened that I had bought a copy at David Mackay's, and I told him so ; but that since it was his original intention to give it to me, I would accept it, and give mine to someone else. He thereon wrote in it, " J. Johnston, from Walt Whitman, July, 1890 "

I afterwards found that he had put the following note on page 53, by the side of Rudolph Schmidt's letter—"This is the letter of R. S.,

Bucke says he has heard him speak of hearing the grass grow, and the trees coming into leaf. In the " Song of Myself " he mentions the " bustle of growing wheat." And, as to scent, he says in " Specimen Days," " There is a scent in everything, even the snow; no two places hardly any two hours, anywhere are alike. How different the odour of noon from midnight, winter from summer, or a windy spell from a still one ! "

referred to by me when Dr. J. asked about the photo in Mickle-street."

Speaking of David Mackay, I mentioned the fact of his being a Scotsman, when he said that he had known quite a number of Scotsmen, "dozens, scores of them," and had a high admiration for them. There was something "very human," something "very good and attachable," in the Scottish people, especially in the mothers of large families. Scotsmen, he thought, were apt to be a little glum and morose, as Carlyle was, but as they became old they usually mellowed a good deal.

I told him I had got an autographed copy of "Peter Peppercorn's" poems, and he said he was glad I had, because he knew "Peter" very well, and liked him for his genuine goodness of heart, and his sharpness of intellect, which was almost "canny." He was a Scotsman, or of Scottish extraction; sometimes came to Camden to see him; and, with all his faults, was a downright good fellow.

Another volume I had was " Poems by Hermes" (Thayer), whom he also knew. "He comes here," he said, "and is a fine fellow —in fact, a very handsome fellow. I believe he is writing a history of modern Italy, including Garibaldi and his times."

He afterwards most willingly consented to let me try to take a photograph of the interior of his room, which I did, but he said,—

"You can't do it, Doctor, no more than you can photograph a bird. You may get an outline of the bird's body, but you can't fix the life, the surrounding air, the flowers, and the grass."

Before leaving, he shook hands very warmly with me, saying,—

"Good-bye, Doctor, good-bye! Give my love to Wallace and the rest of the fellows, and tell them that I hope they won't overestimate Walt Whitman. He doesn't set up to be a finished anything, but just a rough epitome of some of the things in America. I have always been glad to hear from you all, and now that I have seen you *in propriâ personâ* I feel that I know you, and regard you as friends. Good-bye, good-bye!"

His Good-Bye.

Coming downstairs, I was invited by Mrs. Davis to join them in their mid-day repast, which I did; and much did I enjoy the sugared blackberries, bread and butter, and coffee. In fact, I regard it as almost the crowning honour that I should be asked to share the hospitality of Whitman's house, and to sit in that quaint, ship's-cabin-like kitchen, as one of the family.

Mrs. Davis gave me a fan which " Mr. Whitman" used for some time, and had given to her; also a bottle of most beautiful shells (off the mantel-piece), which her late husband had brought from the Island of Cuba. These are presents from Mrs. Davis to Mrs. Johnston.

Another member of the household is Harry Fritzinger—" Warry's " brother—a fine, tall, handsome young American, quiet and reserved in manner, but very likeable, and evidently " a good sort."

The other inmates are Polly the robin, Watch the spotted dog, a parrot, Kitty the black cat, and a canary bird.*

While siting there I was surprised to hear the poet coming downstairs "all by himself," and he actually got nearly to the bottom before Warren could reach him. When he was seated in the front room he asked:

"Has the Doctor gone?"

"No, sir," answered Warren. "He's having a cup of coffee and some blackberries in the kitchen."

"Oh," said Whitman, "I'm very glad, and I hope he'll enjoy them."

We overheard him tell Mrs. Davis that he had sent a poor woman a dollar, and she had just replied, saying that she had "re-

---

* This bird, which was the subject of Whitman's lines, "My Canary Bird," died shortly after my visit, and Mrs. Davis had it stuffed. It was brought to Bolton by Dr. Bucke, together with an autographed copy of the lines, in 1891, and presented to Mr. Wallace.

ceived his gift," which wording did not please him, for he said,—

"Why can't she say that she has received the *dollar* I sent, and not go running the devil round the post by saying that she has received my *gift?*"

I then came into the room for my things, and on my saying "Good-bye" again to him, he held out his hand—this time the left one, simply because it seemed to be the handiest at the moment.

Warren came with me to my hotel, assisted me to pack my box, put it on to the hack, went with me to the station, and even accompanied me in the train to the first station out. In our talk he said that he thought Mr. Whitman had enjoyed my coming to see him, and he had never heard him say anything but what was pleasant in reference to it.

Many of his visitors, he said, seemed to expect him to keep talking about "Shakespeare and poetry" and such-like, all the time; and Mr. Whitman told him that he liked a little of the talk of every-day life occasionally—in fact, as Mr. Whitman once put it, he "liked to be a sensible man *sometimes!*"

The following additional notes may be of interest:— *Additional Notes.*

He does not use tobacco. I should be surprised if he did; I could not imagine Walt Whitman smoking.

He does not use a table for writing, but does it on a pad upon his knee, and he writes slowly and deliberately, but without the least perceptible tremor. He uses a huge penholder and pen, and he seldom blots his writing, preferring to let the ink dry.

He speaks slowly, distinctly, and with forceful and telling emphasis, occasionally hesitating for the right word or expression, but always rounding and completing his sentences in his own way; and I noticed that he frequently made use of phrases and words familiar to me in his books.

I cannot forbear quoting the following interesting *personalia* of him by Dr. Bucke, who has known him intimately for a great many years:

<small>Personalia *by Dr. Bucke.*</small>
"He never spoke deprecatingly of any nationality, or class of men, or time, in the world's history, or feudalism, or against any trades or occupations—not even against any animals, insects, plants, or inani-

mate things; nor any of the laws of nature, nor any of the results of these laws, such as illness, deformity, or death. He never complains or grumbles, either at the weather, pain, illness, or at anything else. He never in conversation, in any company, or under any circumstances, uses language that could be thought indelicate. In fact, I have never known of his uttering a word or a sentiment which might not be published without any prejudice to his fame. He never swears; he could not very well, since, as far as I know, he never speaks in anger, and, apparently, never is angry. He never exhibits fear, and I do not believe he ever feels it. His conversation, mainly toned low, is always agreeable and usually instructive. He never makes compliments; very seldom apologises; uses the common forms of civility, such as 'if you please' and 'thank you,' quite sparingly—usually makes a nod or a smile answer for them.

"He never gossips. He seldom talks about private people, even to say something good of them, except to answer a question or remark, and then he always gives what he says a turn favourable to the person spoken of.

"His manner is invariably calm and simple, and belongs to itself alone, and could not be fully described or conveyed."

Of late years he seems to have changed in two particulars. (1) Mrs. Davis told me that he does not now sing much, whereas singing used to be his favourite amusement. Dr. Bucke speaks of him singing whenever he was alone, whatever he was doing, such as while taking his bath, dressing, or sauntering out of doors. (2) He talks more than he used to do. He certainly talked a good deal to me, and as freely and unconstrainedly as to an intimate and lifelong friend.

VISIT TO BROOKLYN.

At 2-40 p.m. I took train for Brooklyn, which I reached about 6, and went to 79, North Portland-avenue, the residence of Mr. Andrew H. Rome, where I received a most cordial welcome from him and his good wife, who is my wife's cousin.

In our talk, Mr. Rome told me many new and interesting details of Whitman's early life—how he became acquainted with him, and

With Andrew H. Rome.

the difficulties they had with the printing of the first edition of " Leaves of Grass." " Whitman," he said, " always earned his own living, was liked by everybody, was never in a temper, never swore, to his knowledge, but once, and then extremely mildly, at something in a newspaper of which he disapproved ; never spoke disparagingly of anyone or anything; was not then a brilliant conversationalist, though he talks more now, and had the knack of drawing other people on to talk of what they knew best about," etc.

The rest of our conversation was about Annan and Annan folks— for Mr. Rome, like myself, is an Annan man—and much did I enjoy that talk about my dear old home, 3,000 miles away.

I have reason to believe that

Mr. Rome is the friend in Brooklyn referred to on page 25 of Dr. Bucke's book.

Friday, July 18*th.* — Morning gloriously fine. In company with Mr. Rome, who took me through many of the public buildings, I visited the corner of Cranberry and Fulton streets, where Whitman's first edition of " Leaves of Grass " was printed—at Mr. Rome's office. I afterwards crossed the Fulton Ferry to New York ; rode down the whole length of Broadway ; walked back to Brooklyn over the magnificent Brooklyn Bridge, and was much impressed by the superb view over the whole bay, with its splendid shipping, and all the shows of Manhattan—really the finest spectacle of the kind I have ever witnessed, or ever hope to do.

Saturday, July 19th.—Another morning of splendid sunshine, tempered with a gentle breeze.

The "Fulton" Ferry Boat, and John Y. Baulsir.

After a visit in the morning to Coney Island—a favourite haunt of Whitman's in his youth—I spent the afternoon at Fulton Ferry—another of Whitman's youthful haunts—on the boat called the *Fulton*, and there I had another slice of good fortune.

As one of the deck-hands saw that I was going to photograph from the deck, he suggested that I should ask the pilot to allow me to go on the upper deck. This I did, and the pilot's reply was, "I guess you can, if you want to." I gladly went; and, after a little while, we got into conversation, in the course of which I asked him, "Did you ever hear tell of Walt Whitman?"

He looked up quickly and said,

THE "FULTON" FERRY BOAT.

" Do you mean Walt Whitman the poet?"

"Yes," I said, "do you know him?"

" I should think I do!" he replied. " Why, he used to come on this very ferryboat, when I was a young fellow, nearly every day, and go backwards and forwards with us for an hour at a time."

" Indeed," I said. " What was he like at that time? Tell me about him, as I'm much interested in all concerning him. I've been to see him at Camden."

" You have?" he said. " I hear he is very feeble now. When I knew him he was a fine, strappin' fellow, tall, broad-shouldered, and straight; walked with a slow, steady, swing. He was a slow speaker. He did not talk much, and seemed to prefer hearin' other folk talk. He took a long time tellin' a thing, but, when he'd done, you'd know what he meant. He had a kind word for everybody and from everybody, for everybody liked him. *I* have good reason to think well of him, for when I had typhoid fever he used to come every day with fruit and delicacies, and sit with me for an hour or two at a time, when I knew he could ill spare it, as he had his duties to attend to. Yes, I have a very great regard for Walter." (This was the first time I had heard anyone call him "Walter," and he often spoke of him by that name.) " There was a little book of his I used to be very fond of, called ' Leaves of Grass.' Do you know it ? I've heard that some folks don't like him for some of the things in that book ; but they need'nt come around this ferry and say anythin' agin' Walter Whitman."

I asked him to write his name in my book, and I found it to be John Y. Baulsir—one of "the Balsirs" mentioned in "Specimen Days." He said that he had known several of the other pilots mentioned there—John Cole, pilot of the *Union*, who was a pilot yet; George White, Luther Smith; and Bill White, who died suddenly and alone at his post in the very chair in which I was then sitting.

He afterwards told me the following incident which he had witnessed: "Walter" and he went one Sunday morning to Trinity Church, Brooklyn, and Whitman forgot to take off his hat. One of the church officials requested him to remove it, in such a low voice that he did not hear him, and thinking that he was defying him, he deliberately knocked it off, whereupon Whitman stooped down, picked it off the floor, and twisting it into a kind of rope—it was a soft felt—he seized the man by the collar and struck him with it on the side of the head three or four times, and then walked out, followed by the red-faced official, who vowed he would have him arrested.*

I spent a couple of hours in that pilot's wheel-house, chatting to him, looking at the stream of passengers, and enjoying the deliciously sweet breeze from the river, the ceaseless movement, and all the brilliant and varied panoramic shows of "Manhattan from the Bay."

---

* On my afterwards telling this to Mr. John Burroughs' he said it was the only instance he had ever heard of Whitman resenting anything.

WEST HILLS, LONG ISLAND.
WHITMAN'S BIRTHPLACE.

VISIT TO WEST HILLS.

Monday, July 21*st.* — After a delightful visit to some relatives at Wheatley, Long Island, I took train to Huntington Here a letter awaited me from Mr. Herbert Gilchrist. A darkey driver took me in a " Brewster's side-bar wagon " on to West Hills, where, after a little difficulty—for candour compels the admission that the name of Walt Whitman is not so familiar in the neighbourhood as I expected—I found the farm house in which he was born. Alighting, I went up to an elderly, farmer-looking man in the yard.

" Good day to you! Are you Mr. Henry Jarvis ? " I asked.

" I believe I am," he replied.

" Is this the farm where Walt Whitman was born ? " I enquired.

"Walter Whitman? I guess so," he replied.

"Well," said I, "I've come a long way to see this house, and I should much like to stay in the neighbourhood all night if I possibly could."

After a little further talk, he "guessed I could stay there," but in a few minutes his wife came out and said she could not accommodate me. However, after a little persuasive eloquence, she consented to let me stay the night; and here I am, writing this note in the very house—perhaps the very room—in which my grand old hero first saw the light, seventy-one years ago!

A Memorable Evening.

After supper with the family, I spent three delightful hours strolling quietly about the neighbourhood, which is exceedingly picturesque, being richly wooded with most luxuriant vegetation, the roads seeming to cut their way through the dense undergrowth of wood and shrub which lined each side, climbed high up the trees, and completely covered the fences. The evening was gloriously fine—another superb sunset, the sun going down in a cloud of glory, the afterglow flooding the entire western sky with blood-red, crimson, and vermilion colour, shading off into violet, pink, yellow, maize, saffron, and pale lemon—an "artist's despair" sunset, which was followed by a starry night of unusual brilliance and beauty—just such another as I had witnessed at sea —the Milky Way stretching like a great luminous belt right across the star-sprinkled sky, galaxy beyond galaxy, the constellations shining in unsurpassed effulgence, and almost shaming the light of the four-days-old crescent moon.

I wandered on in the waning light until the golden orb sank to rest, when I sat upon a fence, noting the quiet beauty of the scene at "the drape of the day," and listening to the all-pervading music of the crickets, which filled the air with their chirping, until the young katydids began their evensong, and the fire-flies flashed their phosphorescent lights on the grass, the roadway, the trees, and the fences, almost rivalling the stars overhead. I strolled along the road to a point where all insect sounds ceased, and there stood still to absorb the deep solitude and peace, and the sublime spectacle of the luminous, crowded heaven above. I do not remember to have ever experienced such a sense of utter solitude and silence as when I stood there under the silvery radiance of the moon, "alone with the stars." They seemed charged with a new beauty and a new meaning addressed to my individual soul. Long did I stand there, drinking in peace, contentment and happiness and never shall I forget the experience of that solemn "hour for the soul." It is of such a night as this that Whitman writes so beautifully :—

July 22nd, 1878.

"I am convinced there are hours of Nature, especially of the atmosphere, morning and evening, addressed to the soul. Night transcends for that purpose what the proudest day can do. Now, indeed, if never before, the heavens declared the glory of God. It was to the full the sky of the Bible, of Arabia, of the prophets, and of the oldest poems. There, in abstraction and stillness (I had gone off by myself to absorb the scene, to have the spell unbroken), the copiousness, the removedness, vitality, loose-clear-crowdedness of that stellar concave spreading overhead, softly absorb'd into me, rising so free, interminably high, stretching east, west, north, south—and I, though but a point in the centre below, embodying all.

"As if for the first time, indeed, creation noiselessly sank into and through me its placid and untellable lesson beyond—oh, so infinitely beyond!—anything from art, books, sermons, or from science, old or new. The spirit's hour—religion's hour—the visible suggestion of God in space and time—now once definitely indicated, if never again. The untold pointed at—the heavens all paved with it. The Milky Way, as if some superhuman symphony, some ode of universal vagueness, disdaining syllable and sound—a flashing glance of Deity, address'd to the soul. All silently—the indescribable night and stars—far off and silently."—*Specimen Days, pp. 118-119.*

Tuesday, July 22nd.—After a most refreshing night's sleep I awoke to the singing of some sweet little songsters at my window. What they are nobody here can tell me, but they are certainly not English. Even the so-called robin is not the English robin, but seems to be a sort of cross between it and a thrush, being almost as large as the latter, with a red breast and a long spread-out tail, which it flicks about with sharp, sudden, spasmodic jerks, like a blackbird.

I was up betimes, and went out into the grateful morning air and the beautiful sunshine, which flooded and steeped everything with its glory.

I walked, or rather waded, through a field covered with tall, rank grass, wild flowers and weeds, rising almost breast high, and was perfectly amazed at the wealth of rich colour, and the multitudinous abundance and variety of insect life there displayed, the creatures seeming fairly to revel in that field as in an insect paradise. Great club-bodied dragon flies buzzed with their gauzy, diaphanous wings; butterflies of every conceivable tint and hue hovered and fluttered from flower to flower; brown locusts and green grass-

An Insect Paradise.

hoppers shuffled and fiddled on the slender, bending stalks of the tall, golden-headed grasses; yellow-bodied, black-barred bees hummed and sang as they flitted from the nectar-laden chalices; flies, moths and "bugs" of all kinds were there in almost countless numbers; and the katydids were loudly whispering their self-contradictory assertions, that "Katy did," and "Katy didn't." Where could such a scene as that be found but in America?

Soon—too soon, alas, for I was reluctant to leave this charming district, the motherly-kind Mrs. Jarvis and her interesting household—my darkey came along with his wagon, to take me on to Centreport Cove, to visit Mr. Herbert Gilchrist.

On the road we met an old

man named Sandford Brown, who, I had been told, had known Whitman in his youth. We stopped him, and the following are some of the scraps of his talk *re* Whitman:—

My Talk with Sandford Brown.

"Walter Whitman, or 'Walt,' as we used ter call him, was my first teacher. He 'kept school' for 'bout a year around here. I was one of his scholars, and I used ter think a powerful deal on him. I can't say that he was exactly a failure as a teacher, but he was certainly not a success. He warn't in his element. He was always musin' an' writin','stead of 'tending to his proper dooties; but I guess he was like a good many on us—not very well off, and had to do somethin' for a livin'. But school-teachin' was not his *forte*. His *forte* was poetry. Folks used ter consider him a bit lazy and indolent, because, when he was workin' in the fields, he would sometimes go off for from five minutes to an hour, and lay down on his back on the grass in the sun, then get up and do some writin', and the folks used ter say he was idlin'; but I guess he was then workin' with his brain, and thinkin' hard, and then writin' down his thoughts.

"He was a tall, straight man, but not so tall as his father and his uncle, who were about 6½ feet high."

Here I showed him the portrait in "Leaves of Grass," when he said that he did not recognise the features as he then knew them, but he did recognise the negligent style of the dress, the open collar, and the "way of wearin' the hat."

"He kept school for a year," he

went on, "and then his sister"—Fanny, he thought—"succeeded him. I did not see him again for about forty years, when one day he came to my house and asked me,—

"'Do you know anything about Walt Whitman?'

"'I should think I do,' I said. And I looked at him, reco'nisin' him, and said,—

"'Yes, an' I *know* Walt Whitman.'

"'Yes,' said Walt holding out his hand, 'I see you do; but I have seen those that didn't.'

"I'm one of the very few left," continued the old man, "that knew him in the old days, but there are enough on us to be his pall-bearers, and I hope, when his time comes, that he will elect to lie here, where all his forbears rest."

I told him I had seen a newspaper paragraph to the effect that he had selected his burial place in Camden, at which he hung his head, and said sadly,—

"Oh, I'm very sorry if that's so. I've never read his 'Leaves of Grass,' because I could not afford to buy it; but I've heard tell that some folks say some parts of it is immoral; but I can't believe that, because Walt was always a man of strict propriety. But it may be that those folks don't quite understand his meanin'. He is a very well eddicated man, and a very deep thinkin' man, and I am quite sure that he would write nothin' but what he believed to be good, proper, and true. I believe he is far in advance of his time."

"Yes," I said, "he will have to be dead and buried a hundred years before he is properly appreciated."

At this the old man looked suddenly up at me, and said quite sharply,—

"Bury Walt Whitman, did you say? No, sir-r! They'll never bury Walt Whitman! *Walt Whitman'll never die!*"—and he nodded significantly at me, as much as to say, "I have you there!"

"And so," I said, "you believe in the immortality of the soul?"

"Well, naow," he replied slowly, "it would take too long to explain my views on that subject, and I might say somethin' which might mislead you; but I may say I believe that nothin' really dies that has ever lived. I believe, too, that I once existed before I lived in my present form, and that I shall again live as an individual after I have changed my present form."

"Why," I said, "that is something like Whitman's belief."

"I don't know whose belief it is, but I tell you it's mine," he said.

"Walt Whitman is a great favour*ite* of mine, and I think a good deal on him. I don't say that because I know he has now made a name for himself and become famous. Lots of folks want to claim friendship with him now, but I hear he won't have 'em. But it's what I've allus thought, and I would give almost anythin' just to take him by the hand and look in his face—though I wouldn't tell him—oh, dear, no!—I wouldn't tell him—I couldn't tell him, what I think on him!"

VISIT TO MR. HERBERT GILCHRIST.

The remainder of our journey was uneventful, a long drive along the shore of Centreport Cove bringing us to the Moses Jarvis Farm, where Mr. Herbert Harlakenden Gilchrist is located and lives alone—literally so—and does everything for himself—cooking, washing-up, bed-making, etc. The house—an old wooden farm-house, formerly built on the low ground on the shore, but moved up to its present elevation sometime during the war—is commandingly situated on the brow of the hill overlooking the beautiful bay, which Mr. Gilchrist says is like the Bay of Tarsus, and is putting into his new picture. Under his artistic hand, the house has assumed quite a charmingly picturesque and rural-retreat appearance—a sort of ideal artist home. On the walls of the rooms are tacked or pinned various en-

The Moses Jarvis Farm.

gravings, sketches, photographs, etc., notably those of Walt Whitman, his late mother, engravings of some of Rossetti's pictures, a platinotype of his own picture the "Rake's Progress," (exhibited last year), photographs of friends, etc., and on the table a copy of his biography of his mother. A beautiful skin rug covers the luxurious couch in the large room, and in the inner room is a fine old spinning wheel. The kitchen is at the back, and there is a good orchard and garden attached.

I received a most cordial greeting, and an invitation to stay all night with him, which I regretted I could not accept. He was engaged cooking the dinner when I arrived, and it did seem strange to hear this cultured English artist and author say,—

"Excuse me, but I must go and attend to the dinner."

And a real good dinner we had—roast beef, potatoes, spinach, green peas, and stewed apples—all except the beef raised in his own garden, I believe.

I found him a most agreeable host and a pleasant companion. We had an interesting conversation, and it was with extreme regret that I left him to return to Brooklyn in the evening.

VISIT TO MR. JOHN BURROUGHS.

Wednesday, July 23rd. — This morning I left Brooklyn, and sailed up the beautiful Hudson river to West Park, on a visit to Mr. John Burroughs. Our steamer, *The Albany*, was a floating palace, most luxuriously fitted-up, and filled to overflowing with a

Up the Hudson.

thoroughly characteristic American crowd of well-dressed people. We were favoured with ideal weather, and the sail up the magnificent river was most enjoyable, the scenery being of the highest order—somewhat like that of the Rhine, *minus* the castles. The banks beyond the Palisades are beautifully wooded and diversified with houses, villages and towns, most picturesquely nestling among the trees. The beauty is concentrated at West Point, where the scenery is exceedingly fine.

John Burroughs.

Landing at Poughkeepsie, I ferried to West Park, where I found Mr. Burroughs watching some workmen sinking a well through a rock in the grounds of a new house adjoining his own. He is a fine, farmer-like man, of medium height, with a well-built

JOHN BURROUGHS.

frame, a good head, well posed on his square, sturdy shoulders, a long, flowing, grizzled beard and moustache, and greyish hair. His sun-browned face has a peculiarly pleasant expression, especially about the eyes, which twinkle with a merry light when he smiles ; and he has a well-shaped, nearly Roman, nose, a mobile mouth, and a full, broad, rounded forehead.

He was dressed in a free and easy style — grey, home-spun trousers, striped shirt, no vest, a plum-coloured, loose alpaca coat, a white straw hat, and canvas boots ; and is altogether a good-looking fellow, with a genial, likeable presence, and an out-of-door air about him—just such a man as one might expect this cultured lover and critic of nature and of books to be.

In his Summer House.

He gave me a most cordial reception, and took me at once to his summer-house—a shingle-roofed, wooden structure, built of peeled hemlock and vine branches intertwined. It stands at the head of a vine-clad slope, beneath some wide-branching, leafy trees, directly overlooking the Hudson. It is open on all sides, and is provided with a small table, a seat on each side, and a couple of comfortable chairs. Up in one corner near the roof was a last year's robin's nest. On the seat and the table were lying papers, magazines, and books, among which were the "Cultivator," the "Country Gentleman," the "Conservator," the "Critic," the "Chautauquan," the "Unitarian Review," the "Blessed Birds" (by Eldridge E. Fish), "Lorna Doone," "Wide Awake," etc. We sat down, he insisting upon my occupying the most comfortable chair, and had two hours' most enjoyable talk in the delightful shade of that cool retreat, with the trees swaying and sighing overhead, the majestic Hudson smoothly gliding seawards in front of us, the birds singing and fluttering among the trees all around us, and the vines at our feet.

He was, of course, much interested in all I had to tell him about Whitman, and spoke very affectionately about him. He said he had been with him a good deal 20 or 25 years ago, and owed much to him. Whitman, he said, was altogether a unique man—a problem for the future. When he

(J. B.) and W. D. O'Connor began to write about him, there was a good deal of opposition, "pooh-poohing," and ridicule, but now there was a great change in the treatment of him, and he was no longer insulted by the literary guild, as he used to be.

Speaking of O'Connor, he showed me one of his letters, and told me of his death.

"Did you ever know him?" he asked.

"Only through his essay on Whitman," I replied.

His Talk re O'Connor and Whitman.

"Ah!" he said quickly and with emphasis, "*that* was a splendid bit of work, wasn't it? Well, he was one of the most acute-minded men I ever knew. His intellect was like a Damascus blade—so clean-cutting and incisive. He was a vehement debater, and the most brilliant talker I ever heard. He was a great reader, and never seemed to forget anything he read—he had it, apparently, at his finger ends. His essay on Whitman shows him at his best. It is vigorous, trenchant, high-pitched, full of sarcasm, and is unsurpassed. He was a keen controversialist, and Whitman and he used to have some fierce tussles. He held socialistic views, was a great hater of kings and emperors, whom Walt would often defend, and the two of them used to go at it pellmell. I didn't care for these wordy wars, but Walt enjoyed them. He liked to be stimulated, and O'Connor stimulated him—with a vengeance! At that time, Whitman came to my house in Washington regularly every Sunday morning to breakfast, for three or four years. He always came by the street-cars, rolling off and walking down street with a great swing, which was characteristically his own. He was never punctual though, and we had always to wait breakfast for him; he was never methodical in his habits. Mrs. Burroughs used to make very nice buckwheat cakes, of which he was very fond. After breakfast we sat and talked till noon, when he would roll off home, going every Sunday evening to tea to O'Connor's, where I often joined them. He has stayed with me here for weeks at a time, and I've tried to get him to come and live in this neighbourhood—in a cottage close by—which would be far better for him than that half-dead place, Camden, but he isn't to be moved."

In a little while we began to talk about the birds, through my asking him the name of a certain bird near us. It happened to be the king-bird, which, he said, was a remarkable little creature for keeping a place clear of hawks, crows, and such pests, frequently attacking them by getting on to their backs and tweaking their feathers, or otherwise annoying them. He had seen a king-bird on the back of an eagle doing this.

And thus began what was to me one of the most delightful treats I had in America, viz., listening to John Burroughs discoursing upon American birds. While sitting there we saw or heard the following:—The cat-bird (a wonderfully appropriate name, for its call is just like the mewing of a cat), king-bird, wood-thrush, robin, song-

John Burroughs and the Birds.

sparrow (a sweet little songster), goldfinch, swallow, bush-sparrow, and, later on, the phaebe-bird, purple finch—I caught a young one indoors next morning—high-hole, indigo-bird, blue-bird, etc.

One of the most striking things about him was the fact that he recognised every one of them in an instant by their notes—either their songs or their calls—and could at once differentiate each individual bird, even though there might be several together of different species. He would suddenly exclaim:—

"That is the woodthrush with its sweet notes—'pu-ri-ty, holy-be!' There is the song of the phaebe-bird—over there, you may just hear the 'ch-e-e-p' of the blue-bird, and there goes the robin, which is really a thrush," etc., etc.

Later on, I had a sample of his wonderfully acute and accurate powers of observation. While walking down to the Post Office—he is Postmaster—which is in West Park Station, he called my attention to an elm, pointing out how it differed from our English elms, and said, "These long branches overhanging the roadway are favourite nesting places for the oriole, which loves to swing in the wind, and I shouldn't be surprised if we saw one in one of these trees." In a few moments his sharp eyes had detected the very thing he expected, and he exclaimed, "Oh, there's one!" pointing directly to an oriole's nest swaying at the very end of the long branch.

He is a thorough countryman in his habits, rising at what he calls the "ridiculous hour" of five a.m., and going to bed at 9 p.m. He has a farm of about eighteen acres, on which he grows nothing but fruit—apples, pears, raspberries, strawberries, blackberries, peaches, currants, and grapes—for the market. He was much concerned about the apparently imminent failure of his grape harvest, through a black blight which had struck the newly formed grapes. He took me through his grounds—lading me with apples and pears—down to the immense wooden ice-houses by the river side—" our only cathedrals here," he said—and entering them he tried to awake their echoes by shouting " echo ! echo ! " at the top of his voice.

His Fruit Farm.

To a question of mine as to how he did with his vines, fruit trees, etc., during a dry season, he replied, " They have just to take

their chance and wait until the rain comes." "Do you never water them?" I asked. (There is a natural spring of beautifully clear and good-tasting water in his grounds). "No," he replied, "We cannot imitate Nature's method, which is slow, gentle, and penetrating. Ours is too rapid, and soddens the soil, instead of moistening it gradually through and through as rain does."

On our return he took me into his study—a two-windowed, square, one-storey building, situated a few yards behind the summer-house. The walls outside are covered with large strips of bark. Entering this *sanctum*, we find two sides of it devoted to well-filled book-shelves let into the wall; a strong, well-cushioned couch stands on one side, and near the door is an open

His Study.

fireplace with hearth, for a wood fire, a gun resting against the jamb. In the centre of the room are one or two chairs, and a large, substantial table, all littered with books, papers, magazines, pamphlets, etc., a good reading-lamp standing in the centre. Another table beneath the bookshelves is covered with books, among which were cloth bound copies of David Douglas's edition of his own six little volumes, while stacked in the corners are piles of periodicals, manuscripts, etc. Pinned or tacked on the walls, or resting on the mantelpiece, are portraits of Walt Whitman—two or three of these, —Matthew Arnold, Humboldt, Carlyle, Emerson—these two last similar to the ones that used to be in J. W. Wallace's room at Eaglestreet—Lyell, Ibsen—he has not got the Ibsen mania,—Thoreau, and others, including the profile of himself which appeared in *The Century*. There are also several pictures of birds, an oriole's nest in which the birds had interwoven some coloured yarn, a gigantic moth, and a good many other natural curiosities.

From the study we went into his house, where I was introduced to the hospitably-kind Mrs. Burroughs and to their boy. The house, which was planned by himself, is built upon sloping ground, so that it has three-storeys behind and two in front. It has four gables, a porch in front, and a spacious balcony behind commanding a splendid view across the waters of the Hudson and its richly-wooded and fertile banks away to "the delectable moun-

His House.

tains." The house is mainly built of stone—a dark-grey, quartz-veined slate, quarried in the neighbourhood ; and in showing it to me Mr. Burroughs remarked, "Who would build with brick when they could get such stone as that close at hand?" The upper storey is of wood, and the greater part of the front is covered by the red foliage of the Virginia vine. The interior is most charming, the whole of the wood-work from floors to rafters being different natural-coloured woods, carefully arranged so as to contrast and yet harmonise with each other, and the carpets and wall papers are all toned low, and in pleasing combinations of colour.

After supper—the Americans call our "tea" supper—we returned to the summer-house, where we sat talking and watching the long raft-tows slowly gliding down the river, until the light faded, the fire-flies lit their flashing lamps, the tree crickets fiddled and chirruped out their monotones, and the stars twinkled overhead through the trees.

Thursday, July 24th.—I arose at 6 a.m., and spent a most delightful time with Mr. Burroughs in his grounds, study, and summer-house —our talk being mainly about America and England, their poets, literary men, and literature. He has a sweetly-toned, well modulated voice, with a clear, musical ring in it. He talks well and fluently, and there is a marked individuality about some of his sentences and phrases which a student of his writings could easily detect.

His Talk re Poets.

The poet who is more to him than any other is Wordsworth, and next to him comes Tennyson. The latter, he thinks, is more fluent, more universal than Wordsworth, and is undoubtedly a great poet. To him Tennyson's great charm lies in his universality and his sympathy.

"Browning," he said, "I cannot read with any satisfaction. He is very brilliant, very clever, very scholarly, but he is all the time striking verbal attitudes—like someone turning somersaults over chairs. It's very clever, no doubt; but gracious! It tires me to think of it! He has not voiced his age like Tennyson. I like a poet who draws me with cords of sympathy and love, rather than one who is astonishing me all the time with his verbal contortions. I do not respond to Browning; he seems to require some trait of which I am deficient."

The younger generation of English poets are, he remarked, a long way behind; and the same is true of the American. Swinburne he abominates. Morris and Dobson have written some good things, but none which appeal to his deeper nature. There are none to take the places of Longfellow—some of whose things "will keep," as he phrases it—Bryant, Emerson, and Whittier. Oliver Wendell Holmes is very clever and very witty, but there is nothing solid, helpful, moulding, or formative about his writing.

He deplores the present state of literature in America, from the newspapers upwards.

"In America," he said, "there is a host of authors and poetlings.

In New York there is a 'Society of Authors,' of which I was a member; but some two or three years ago they actually blackballed Whitman! I've never been inside the doors since that. They would have done themselves infinite honour had they elected him—*I* didn't propose him,—but they showed themselves contemptible little fools by refusing him. They are mostly second-rate, obscure scribblers, who consider themselves poets—and Whitman is not a poet, in their opinion!"

He spoke a little about his private life—said he had very few friends in the neighbourhood for whom he really cared much, his neighbours being mostly rich merchants who knew nothing about books. He was engaged most of his time on his farm; and spent most of his leisure in his summer-house or study, ever since a slight illness a year or two ago, which made him resolve to live mostly out-of-doors; but he often wished he had some congenial society, and that he could see Whitman now and then. He was sure it would do him a lot of good.

On my showing him the large portrait which Whitman had given to me for Mr. Wallace, he exclaimed, — "Gracious! That's tremendous! He looks Titanic! It's the very best I have yet seen of him. It shows power, mass, penetration, *everything*. I like it too because it shows his head. He *will* persist in keeping his hat on and hiding the grand dome of his head. The portrait shows his body too. I don't like the way so many artists belittle their sitters' bodies."

Re *the Gutekunst Portrait.*

"What a magnificent head it is!" he again exclaimed. "Every part of it large and in perfect proportion. It is built like a splendid stone bridge—every part necessary, and the whole perfect in symmetry. It is certainly the very finest head, and Whitman is the greatest all-round personality that this country has yet produced.

SUPPLEMENTARY NOTES.

Such are some of the details I learned about Walt Whitman during my short visit to America; but interesting and perhaps valuable as they are, I feel that they form but an imperfect record of an experience which is indelibly graved into my memory as one of the most important events of my life.

When I think with what open-

> Camden New Jersey U S America
> Dec: 2 '90 — the <u>Notes</u> & Good Words have come all right — Of the <u>Notes</u> I wd like you to send a copy each to
> Mrs: O'Connor, 112 M street N.W. Washington DC
> Mrs. Mary E Van Nostrand Greenport, Suffolk Co New York
> Miss Whitman 2436 2d Carondelet Av St Louis Missouri
> Mrs: H L Heyde, 21 Pearl street, Burlington Vermont
> R G Ingersoll, 45 Wall street New York city
> Sloane Kennedy Belmont, Mass
> David McKay, Publisher, 23 south 9th St Philadelphia
> Talcott Williams, Press newspaper office, Philadelphia } U S America
>
> Bernard O'Dowd Supreme Court Library, Melbourne Victoria
> R Pearsall Smith 44 Grosvenor Road, Westminster Embankm't London
> Edwd Carpenter, Millthorpe near Chesterfield Eng
> M Gabriel Sarrazin magistrat Nouméa Nouvelle Caledonie (Colonies Françaises)
> ? to Tennyson
> W M Rossette Euston Square London
> J Addington Symonds Davos Platz, Switzerland
>
> Have read the <u>Notes</u> all through & accept & like them (am pleased & flatter'd always in the best human side) — hope you have had a good lot struck off by the printer as they will surely be wanted — & (barring their fearfully eulogistic tinge) I endorse all —
>
> Walt Whitman

Reduced *Facsimile* of Portion of Whitman's Letter.

hearted loving-kindness he received me, with what open-handed generosity he treated me, what trouble he took to please me—allowing me to photograph himself and his surroundings, ransacking his treasures for souvenirs—" somethings for tokens "—of his great love; giving me an oil-painting of himself, two autograph photographs and six autograph books for J. W. Wallace and myself—when I think of the hours of unconstrained, genial, friendly talk I had with him, and the homely intimacy to which I was admitted—when I think of his considerate kindness in writing to Bolton after my first visit, and of his tenderly anxious, almost paternal, solicitude concerning me, after I left him, because he had not heard from me—when I think of the many tokens of his regard that we have been favoured with since my return—above all, when I think of the immense debt I owe him through his books, my heart fairly swells with reverent, grateful affection to that superbly grand old man, that large, sweet soul, "exhaling love as a dew," who is to me the ideal of humanity, the living embodiment of all that is manly, noble, heroic, wholesome, kind, and essentially lovable in our nature.

He is by far the most impressive personality I ever came in contact with. Jove-like in his majesty, he is childlike in his simplicity, and pre-eminently natural and unaffectedly sincere through every fibre of his being.

He is like a piece of primeval, out-of-door nature itself: shaggy, untrimmed, majestic, picturesque, as of a piece with the cliffs, the sea, the mountains, and the prairies; and he has the charm and influence of Nature herself, tonic and life-giving. It is impossible, I think, for anyone to look upon his noble face, to take him by the hand, to walk and talk with him, to listen to the tones of his sweetly melodious voice, and to gaze into the azure depths of his blue-grey eyes without feeling drawn to him by that irresistible magnetic attraction which makes almost everyone like him at once. He is the impersonation of all those qualities which constitute *Cameraderie*—nay, he *is Cameraderie*. He seems to irradiate an all-encompassing sympathy like an aroma, so that one wishes to be always with him, and feels loth to leave him.

www.ingramcontent.com/pod-product-compliance
Lightning Source LLC
Chambersburg PA
CBHW030344170426
43202CB00010B/1230